A JOURNEY
TOWARD **WHOLENESS**
THROUGH A PROCESS OF
CONFLICT * CHANGE * CONVERSION

Philip J. Klauder Jr. M.S.

WESTBOW
P R E S S®
A DIVISION OF THOMAS NELSON
& ZONDERVAN

WestBow Press books may be ordered through booksellers or by contacting:

WestBow Press
A Division of Thomas Nelson & Zondervan
1663 Liberty Drive
Bloomington, IN 47403
www.westbowpress.com
1 (866) 928-1240

Scripture taken from Douay-Rheims Version of the Bible.

ISBN: 978-1-9736-7208-1 (sc)
ISBN: 978-1-9736-7207-4 (hc)
ISBN: 978-1-9736-7209-8 (e)

Library of Congress Control Number: 2019911930

Print information available on the last page.

WestBow Press rev. date: 9/17/2019

SECTION I

PROLOGUE OF MY ADDICTION IN A CHRONOLOGICAL ORDER

My name is Phil K and I'm a recovering alcoholic. This is my story! This narrative is a 1st person account of my life emanating from the first day that I sipped booze. I am vague on the day, but my relatives gave me sips of beer occasionally and I enjoyed it. The truth that you are not an alcoholic until you take your first drink, in my case, my first sip.

Sips were much more common and I remembered eating maraschino cherries laced with a Manhattan cocktail. Well, that was great and I loved the taste, but more importantly, I loved the "buzz". (buzz means you are relaxed and leads to mind altering euphoria). Although, it was brief!

My family of origin were abusive drinkers, my mother and my father together with close relatives, aunts and uncles.

There are three classes of drinkers:

(1) **Social**, one who takes a drink or two in a social setting.

(2) **Abusive**, one who imbibes in a drink, two or more leading to a buzz.

(3) **Dependent**, one who is defined as a loss of control, a person who is addicted to alcohol, functional or

dysfunctional. But, the progression of the disease leads to a chronic state of physical and emotional turmoil ends in infirmity or death.

My father was an alcohol and he died when he was sixty-two. In 1967, he was diagnosed with stomach cancer and his life was riddled in alcohol episodes which adversely affected me emotionally. As the first child among five, I was the hero child and affected my fathers' drunken rants. He drank daily and he lost multiple jobs, but many of his enablers were in his own family sisters, brothers especially my mother. They didn't know what to do because it was an age when alcohol recovery was a distant thought. They didn't understand 'tough love' because tough love is a means to the end of stopping the endless drunken cycles of abuse and torment to the alcohol and his dysfunctional family. I, the hero child, wanted to protect my family and, in turn, I hated the behavioral results of alcohol.

Alcohol is a biological disease and once you inherit the gene; it can't be controlled, but understanding of the disease concept gives hope in recovery. Although, the biological cause is in your nature, but the personal development is the culminating effect whether or not, you will become an alcoholic.

CHAPTER 1

TEENAGE YEARS

I drank beer often, but I was not yet affected by 'out of control' drinking. I remember when I was sixteen, I used an altered date on my driver's license. I looked like I was twelve, a skinny and blond kid accompanied when a friend who looked like eighteen went into a down and out bar. It was beyond the tracks in Juniata Park, and their clientele were drunks and wannabe drunks. The bar keeper carded me and a friend and I drank beer for hours. I noticed there was a pit or a gully on the floor lying beneath our stools. I inquired to the bartender about it? He stated that it was a spittoon, where you actually spit to the floor. This day was a vomitorium and I learned my lesson for a few days because I was so sick. I was flagged by that place, but no one knew about it except my friend.

I, really did not drink during school days but I drank on weekends. My parents didn't observe my drinking because they were drinking heavily and they were oblivious to me. I was a functional student.

In my senior year of high school, I was seventeen, my class was taken to Washington D.C. on a bus along with two priests who escorted us. I had been suspended because I cut my first class, and I spent weeks JUG (Justice under God), a place where you spent time after class accounting for your misdeeds. I was in a class of boys and I was now acting out. I had no behavioral issues, but the disciplinarian told me that, I had senioritis, his word to describe an inflated sense of self, thinking that you made it to your senior year, but in reality you did not.

A month before, I used my fake driver's license to purchase a bottle of the cheapest wine. It was called Thunderbird and I carried the bottle secretly to the bus. I was seated in the back and I popped the cork. I was an instant celebrity and the boys in the back of the bus were treated. It was only one bottle and none of the priests knew what was going on. But, in hindsight, they might have carried their flasks, but who knows?

The case in point that I was acting out ♀ alcoholically. I was not drunk, but I was acting irresponsibly. If I was caught, I might have been expelled. What a risk for me? I was an honor's student and I never thought about the consequences. It was all about me. The narcissistic traits were part of my alcoholic behavior. It continued sporadically throughout my teens.

My graduation in High School was a special day. I graduated from the honor's stage and the ensuing party was attended by many of the Oblate priests who were friends of my father and uncles. I remembered a conversation with a priest. We called him "Sleepy Charlie". He was my freshman religion teacher but he slept throughout the class. Anyway, he was brilliant guy and I loved to talk to him about philosophy and theology especially in the wee hours of the night. Both of us were alcoholics, talking the talk but not walking the walk.

I entered the Oblate of St. Francis de Sales novitiate in Childs, Maryland. Because of my immaturity, I left the seminary after a few months. They didn't throw me out, but I could not handle the discipline and I left on my own. This is when I learned in recovery that I was a misguided person, an immature young man who was in 'Conflict' between his true and false self. The self was split psychologically between his superego (conscience) and his id (basic urges). A person, or an acknowledged alcoholic, is torn between their higher nature and the lower nature. That was developing in my unconscious psyche and I learned much from my recovering alcohol days and my educational experience in my late forties and early fifties.

CHAPTER 2

TWENTIES

My twenty-first birthday was spent at United States Marine Corps boot camp, Parris Island, South Carolina. I spent thirteen weeks there and it was the most challenging thing in my life.

I had enlisted in the Marine Corps for six years, six months in active duty and the balance was in the active reserve. The reason that I was enlisted because I was fascinated with the Marine Corps and their dedication to discipline. For which I had none. I used to say that I was crystallizing my thoughts, but the real reason was I was an emotional mess.

I challenged myself because I was tormented by my unstable life. I began college at Saint Joseph's University. I only lasted for one semester. I didn't have any money to follow through and I lost interest in college. I drank beer when I could and I finally decided to go to USMC. I was dating a girl at that time, I took her to a friend's wedding, but I had a drunken argument with her. I left the wedding hall and I staggered five miles and I got lost. I remember this evening because I could have died. It was early winter and I fell asleep in a field and it was very cold. Of course, I never thought at the drunken moment about taking the girl home. I found out the next day that one of my friends drove her home. Since I was a wannabe alcoholic, my behavior was extremely erratic. I knew from my days of recovery that God's Divine Providence took care of me. I was manipulate but this girl was naive. A month later, she accommodated me to my farewell party going into the Marines.

It was difficult for me at Parris Island, USMC boot camp especially emotionally. I was overwhelmed since I had no prior discipline and the drill instructors noticed that I was contrary. Actually, I was so full of anxiety that it was more accidental than deliberate. In one instance, my senior D.I. (drill instructor) noticed that I was drilling (marching) well and he allowed to carry the Guidon (carrying flag and the leading the platoon). Well, that lasted for a few days and my senior D.I. observed that I hadn't shaved in one day. That was a major rule of the Corps, in that, we needed to shave and shower every day.

I decided not to shave that AM because I was late thinking that I was a light skinned blond and no one would have noticed. He noticed it and he delivered me a major take down. He removed my position of leading the platoon and he told me that I needed to march behind the platoon. That lasted for a week or two, but, I never regained my earlier status. In fact, the D.I told me unequivocally: If I forgot to shave again, he will shave me using glass. I learned that lesson in the hard way.

It was a stressful time and I persevered during the thirteen weeks. I graduated from boot camp but the family never attended since it was too far. It was a hurtful day for me. I was alone but there was no celebration because the recruits had no time in boot camp. I didn't have a drink until my advanced infantry training at Camp Geiger, NC. Then we had weekends off and I drank often at the enlisted club.

I made a pledge to God that I would go back to the seminary after I completed my active duty. It was a commitment to God because I needed His Help to get through the rigors of boot camp. Within days of my six month active, I received permission from the Marines to re-enter the Oblate seminary.

I spent a full semester attending Catholic University, freshman year at the seminary's satellite campus. I spent seven months at the seminary and I left on my own. I was a very religious guy which my faith sustained, but I had no real vocation. I remembered one day when I was in Elton, Maryland, a friend told me that I was looking at a liquor store front and my Novice Master passed by and he saw me. I didn't go into the store, but my mind was preoccupied with mundane things.

Once I left the seminary, I was full of myself. I had gained weight and I was not a skinny kid. I had confidence and an 'attitude'. I remembered one girl that I had known and she was a younger friend. She knew my strengths and weaknesses. While talking to her, she asked me, "How are you doing"? I'm sure it was a pompous answer, but her retort was simple. "PJ, you have a superiority complex".

I was twenty-two and she was nineteen, but she had more sense and instincts than I ever had. I never thought about it, but I realized in my after-care that I was masking myself. I was acting out through alcohol and errant behavior. I was an inferior person, an immature guy.

This is my 'false self'. I am an introspective person who needed alcohol to behave in a superior manner. Once I sobered up, I hated myself and hated my drunken ways. Remember, I was in my early twenties sic 1962, and there were no drugs or no sexual revolution which began in the late sixties. It was "Spartan Life" compared to this age. There was much anxiety, repression and spiritual issues. Since I was a religious and spiritual person, I drank in order to repress and suppress my inner thoughts. If I sinned then I would go to confession and I didn't miss Mass weekly.

Even though, my father was an alcohol, he came from a religious family. He was one of nine. His youngest brother was a Salesian priest and his elder sister was a Visitation cloistered nun. They often prayed for my father, but his family enabled him much like my mother. Dad was a good and decent man but his life was replete in lost opportunities. I'm sure he hated himself, but, unlike me, he didn't get external alcohol support. I hated my father, but, in my recovery in 1987, age forty-seven, I made amends with my father. I visited his grave site at Holy Sepulchre Cemetery outside Philadelphia and I cried and I instantly forgave him because he was a sick and troubled person. I understood that he had a chronic and progressive disease and he never had a real opportunity in recovery. His family knew him well, but they were abusive drinkers (counter dependents) or enablers (co-dependents). He died young and he had lost his wife and his family. That was his suffering in earth and, I believe, he's in Heaven.

I met my wife, Rita in the summer of 1963 in a dance-bar in Margate, NJ. I was drinking, no doubt about it, but I asked her to dance then I asked her to give me her phone number which she resisted. She told me, subsequently, that I was a strange person. I wore a clam digger outfit with a rope attached to my waist.

I remembered her name, Rita S. a pretty brunette with brown eyes. She lived in South Philly and I was infatuated with her because she was an independent person and she didn't care about superfluous talk. I was attracted to her candor and sense of well-being. In fact, she had many virtues unlike me and in years to come she gave me spiritual inspiration to accept things that I can change.

But, I never had her number, but I remembered her last name and I researched a phone directory in order to find her parent's number in South Philly. I called her and she was reluctant to talk to me, let along, go out with me.

I spent an hour attempting to cajole her to go out to a date. Finally, she stated that we could do a double date. Her girlfriend liked a guy that I knew. Consequently, we went on a double date, but my friend didn't want to go out with her friend. On my own, I substituted another friend which I bribed him with a case of beer. Anyway, I told Rita and her friend that the other guy was sick and I didn't want to cancel the date.

Rita accepted my first apology and I have innumerable apologies over the years. It was an upbeat date and she understood that I was not strange, and she agreed to go to the second date with me. In hindsight, God's Will was displayed again. Rita was an inspiration and a spiritual gift to me. In the beginning, she was very quiet, but she listened to me and I was attracted to her personally. She had a mystique about her. She had an allure of innocence, goodness and spirituality and once she talked; it all made sense. It all came to fruition despite many arguments in the interim. We were married a year later and my gratitude to God that we persevered. I continued to drink and other arguments exacerbated our personal relationship.

However, I loved her and I committed myself to her and our growing family. I went back to college

11

and received my Bachelors' Degree in 1969 at La Salle College attending four years in nights and Saturdays. Simultaneously, I had a good cost accounting position at General Electric in King of Prussia, PA.

I was drinking abusively in different situations, but I was not drinking alcoholically yet, meaning I was not out of control. Rita tolerated the drinking, in time, it took a toll on our marriage. She enabled me and she stifled herself emotionally. That's one of my regrets in my life. The goodness and love of our hearts is the binding connection between us, our shared sacraments and commitment to God and family.

CHAPTER 3

THIRTIES

Our daughter, Christine, was born in May of 1970. It was a great day for all of us. The day started in early AM which Rita had intense labor pains. I rushed her to the hospital which was an hour away. I stayed with her and her OB doctor told me that it might be few more hours for delivery. My sister's wedding was planned at 11 AM and I was in the wedding party. I talked to Rita and our mutual choice was to attend my sister's wedding.

My father was still alive, but he was not invited to attend my sister's wedding. My sister Sallianne and Bob T. made a mutual decision. In hindsight, their decision was appropriate, but it must have been very difficult for my father to stay away. That's a realistic consequence for not letting go and not letting God help the alcoholic who ignored the intervention of family members.

After the wedding ceremony, I called from a pay phone and I found that Rita delivered a baby girl that early afternoon. We were hoping that God would bless us with a healthy baby girl. I remember stating that "I hit a home run today". It was wonderful day, but drinking started at the afternoon reception; thereafter the wedding party decided to visit Rita at the hospital, an hour away. I drove eight to ten people in my car and we were all drunk. The moral of this story is that I have been so blessed and a tragedy averted since I was driving erratically throughout the city, but we got it to the hospital in one piece. I made dumb decisions and I, thankfully, received God's Divine Providence in getting through that day🙏. 🖤.

Meaningful recovery from alcohol and drugs come from gratitude. If you don't consider the full picture of life and live your day without contrition and appreciation then you live wantonly, an illusory self who takes anything but you give nothing in return. Alcoholic are selfish and self-centered narcissists who don't respect boundaries. It's always about ME!

My life in my thirties was chaotic and I had a good position at GE. I drank abusively especially on the weekends, then I started to develop relational problems at work. I developed an 'attitude' and I left GE and few more positions. But, I was a conniving and controlling person. I decided that I decided to pursue self-employment.

I decided to buy a business which Rita agreed with that decision. Rita has never been vocal in opposition on personal affairs and she trusted me with my business choices unlike my drinking situations. Now, you have to understand that I was educated in accounting and business administration. I had the energy, initiative and capital to pursue the goal with Rita's approval. I made a bank loan and an Uncle lent me the deposit monies to buy a small trucking business. I didn't know anything about the transportation business. My brother, Frank, had a serious heart attack while on duty at the Philadelphia Police Department. Thankfully, he recovered after few months and he received a total disability from the police department. He then joined with me at the trucking company and he had great sense of organization and coordination. I ran the business side and Frank oversaw the operation. I purchased the Goodwill of the previous company and we developed over the years, but my drinking continued unabated and most of the time, I would go to work in the afternoon and leave in the evening. Frank was the morning guy and I was the afternoon guy. Also, I was drinking during the week and weekends. I was a Bon Vivant- in French, a good sociable lifestyle. Moreover, I was a local political committeeman, a founding member of the Horsham Lion's Club and a host of social endeavors.

Alcohol is a chronic, progressive disease. It takes time to unfold and my family suffered from alcohol emotional abuse. An analogy is a wheel; you have the hub and the spokes and a well functional wheel going around and around. If the one of the spokes is misaligned then you have a faulty wheel. It's like a family who is the core and the hub. If you are a healthy family- emotional and physical, then you have a troubled or dysfunctional then you have unhealthy family. You might have exterior and interior love for each other, but things are not right and unconditional love is replaced by the four R's, namely; rage, rejection, resentment and rebellion.

Our youngest son, David, was born in 1974 and now we had four children. Yes, I was preoccupied with work, family, but my primary preoccupation was alcohol. At this point, I tried to moderate my drinking. During lent as a Roman Catholic, I abstained from alcohol for six weeks. On, Easter Sunday arrived, I got drunk.

Let me describe the term 'drunk'. It might have different meanings to many. I was drunk in social setting because I drank two to three Manhattan cocktails, ten to fifteen beers and two to three Sambuca's liqueur. I didn't stagger, but I did slur my words.

I was content in my drunken stupor. I would be belligerent in my behavior towards others. I experienced the stimulated highs of the drink. The following day was full of anxiety, anger, sickness and melancholy. Why would one drink, in order to experience the highs and lows? It's an uncontrollable disease!

I had two outstanding occasions among many when my Good Lord saved me. In one occasion, I was attending a ladies pro-am golf tourney, in Horsham, PA along with my political friends. We were part of this Perry Como pro classic. I was drinking the whole day stashing beer cans in my golf bag, in fact, I left out golf clubs in order to make room for more beer.

After the round of golf and drinking, I decided to abscond the golf cart, but it was a local TV cart with cameras. I, my drunken friends, drove the cart across the golf course attempting to interview professional while golfers. Of course, there was no live feed to the station, but we told the people it was a live interview and after that, we drove the golf cart onto the public road. We were heading to a local pub, but a Horsham cop whom we knew escorted us back to the gold course. Everything was a joke and nothing happened. We should have been arrested, but we were so called politicians. Well it's was a joke on me since my drinking time was working against me. My alcoholic tirades were unchallenged by authorities at this time.

Another occasion while hanging out with the political motley crew, I left my car in a gated part of the Navy base in Horsham. I was supposed to retrieve my car after a party; otherwise, the gates would be locked subsequently. I arrived back after three hours, I noticed that my car was locked inside of the military base.

Given my drunken propensity to amuse myself or others, I decided to climb the fence separating the public from the military installation. I was walking around on an isolated road trying to retrieve my car. But, I never occurred to me in this drunken moment, how will I leave the base? Now, I noticed that vehicle headlights were coming down the road and then I climbed up a tree in order to avoid the vehicle. At that time, the idiotic political friends who were witnessing the situation, now they are pointing at the vehicle and they urged the military police to stop. Idiotically, they told them that a guy was in a tree. Well, things backfired, the MP'S (U.S. Marine military police) removed their 45's and they told me in no uncertain terms, get out of the tree! As this point, I was really high - no pun suggested- in the tree and I couldn't hear them. Then one of my idiot friends told them to shoot me. I could have been shot, once again, I was saved again by Divine Providence and prayers that were offered for my salvation. Consequently, things got serious and the motley crew told the MP's that my car was locked in side of the base, in the meanwhile, I got out of the tree and the MP's wanted to arrest me. Finally, I told them that we were all political people in Horsham and I showed them my U.S. Marine I.D. I was now inactive reservist, but they took me back to the base. The sergeant of the guard and certain of the political people arrived and they let me go. The MP's took me back to my car and escorted me off the Navy base. It was unbelievable story and that story was repeated in local bars by me and my political jerks for years. Yes, SHOOT HIM!

Can you imagine that scenario in this day and age? God has protected me throughout the decades and my forties will be a decade of reckoning!

CHAPTER 4

FORTIES

My forties were a tumultuous epoch of my life. It started in 1980 when my wife, Rita, and our four children moved in our new custom home along with ten acres in Horsham, Pennsylvania. I was drinking, but my political days were gone. I could stand dealing with local politics and the charlatans who were involved. In reality, I had experienced a couple incidents. The ward leader asked me to dump my committee woman for whom I respected. He didn't like her because she was anti-development which was the township sentiment at the time. I told him that I wasn't going to confront her and it was up to him. Well, he confronted her and my political days were numbered. In fact, I finished my election term and I had no other interest in politics. Moreover, a police officer and a drinking friend of mine has purchased a bar and go-go joint in Horsham. Around the same time, I was told that my cop friend left his bar in the wee hours of the morning and he was in route to his home then he struck a tree and died instantly. I could have been with him and it was a sobering time for me. His wife was young and they had three young girls. It was very sad for all.

I was still drinking but my life hanging out with the other drunks was severely curtailed. Rita and I has argued over my drinking and I would make promises to her. Then I stopped for weeks. Finally, after one drinking incident, I stopped on my own in the spring of 1983. I was forty-three and I had no real knowledge of the disease. I knew that I was creating chaos in my life and I needed to stop drinking. The ensuing couple months were terrible and I was a dry drunk. But, my relationship with Rita improved. She didn't drink other than a glass of wine.

I was still involved with my business and I was extremely fortunate that my brother, Frank who supported me in my quest for sobriety. He, too, liked to drink beer, but he was not an alcohol. He enabled me and I, in turn, manipulated him.

Since my drinking stopped, Rita and I helped with charities in the morning or early afternoon, we drove cancer patients to and from Abington hospital for chemotherapy. After work, I volunteered in a Philadelphia homeless center where we delivered food to the homeless. That was a trying time because the homeless had serious mental and alcohol problems. They lived in empty boxes while rats were scurrying around and one day this delusional person attacked another person with a pen knife in my presence. I disarmed him and the police came and they let him go. One cop told me that it's par for the course and the streets in Philadelphia were full of alcoholic Schizophrenias'. The de-institutionalization of neurotics and psychotics began in the early 1970's and the homeless was pervasive in the inner cities.

In 1985, I was still a dry drunk but I decided to go back to graduate school wherein I majored in Pastoral Counseling. This was a combined discipline of psychology and theology. Given my innate interest in spirituality and my personal struggle with "self"; it was a balanced academic curriculum.

I was taught by three licensed psychologists PhD's. I learned fundamentals of counseling, group therapy, spirituality and psychopathology. That latter course was my favorite and I learned a lot of personality characteristics.

In the spring of 1986, my trucking business was growing into warehousing and other pursuits. Then I decided to branch out by retrofitting a forty foot empty trailer. Rita and I were exercising three times a week in Holy Redeemer's hospital exercise facility. At that time, I proposed an idea to the clinical director of a local hospital, whereby I would renovate a forty foot trailer into offices and place an on board power generator. I hired a designer and modeled the interior and exterior of the unit. I made a presentation to the hospital's executive board by naming my organization Most Health Services. This organization's business plan was to offer medical services like corporate fitness, sports psychology, exercise physiology and routine testing like mammograms, blood tests and stress tests.

My company's trucking business would lease a tractor who would haul the trailer from one site to another. My initial investment would be $40,000 and I offered a $20,000 price to the hospital, in addition, I would receive $2,000, part time, four hours a day or sixteen hours a month to begin the sales marketing.

Remember, I was not drinking and my emotional state was in turmoil. The more verbal gratification, I received, the more I became narcissistic, I was strutting my stuff. The hospital accepted my offer and without a written contract, they gave me $20,000 before they saw the finished product and they gave me $2,000, part time once again, no contract with me. Within three months, the trailer was completed by sub-contractors and I was determined to make this venture a success. However, it was not God's plan for me.

The trailer was delivered to their medical facility. Everyone loved the trailer. It was painted black outside with colorful logos and hospital's name was painted large letters on the outside. In fact, an enterprising sports trainer, Jim C was a partner at the hospital working with them on sports conditioning. I had met with him and his business partner early on. He liked the concept but he never followed up with me. His only contribution was that he suggested to the executive board that he favored 'black color' on the trailer. He never helped me, but I didn't need his help. This was 'my deal' and my emotional state was in turmoil. I thought that I was a rock star with the hospital's staff and my sober days were numbered given my insatiable need for attention.

Thereafter, my superiority complex took hold of me. In three years, Rita and I were doing charitable things. Now, I'm distracted by mundane things.

Rita is an emotional rock, and she told me right from the start; you need humility. Well, I never sought humility and it was the opposite for me. I became a narcissistic fool, full of myself and I began drinking in the summer of 1986. Rita was very upset and she has an uncanny ability to understand the good and the bad of situations. She is a very spiritual person and she knew intuitively that things would collapse in due time. I started drinking moderately within months, I was out of control. That's the marker of an alcoholic.

That's why alcoholism is a disease and once you start drinking the progressive nature takes hold of you. Even though, it was three years of sobriety, things went down in months. I was still trying to maintain my part time sales position at the hospital. It was utter madness and it was December, 1986, I was drinking the whole day and night. I arrived at the hospital's clinical lab and I proceeded to trash the office of the director. He was not there and some of the technical staff knew me cleaned up the office and told me to leave. I was irritated at him because he told other executives that I was not fulfilling my responsibilities.

I lost my interest and integrity. I wasn't able to get sufficient clients for the hospital to maintain their profitability. Following that episode, I went into a seven day de-toxification unit in Warminster Hospital. A month later, in January, 1987, I continued to drink heavily and my counselor told me that I was not listening to him. He suggested that I should meet a doctor who specialized in Drug and Alcohol counseling. He was a recovering alcohol and Christian minister. He met with me and he directed me to go a twenty-eight day rehabilitation in Caron Foundation. I understood that I needed help at one level, but my alcoholic self-did not want to go. Rita told me that if I didn't go to Caron Foundation, then pack my bags because I couldn't live at our home. That was tough love ❤ and I went into rehab. I hated it there. Since I was always rebellious, I couldn't unpack my bags for two weeks. I wanted to leave, I prayed fervently to stay put. Within weeks, I became acclimated to the routine. I enjoyed the therapy group sessions and I learned about my disease. Finally, I addressed the full group in the rehab. I finally unpacked my bags and the group applauded me. Now, it was a turning point in my recovery. The final two weeks of the rehab was much better. I complied with the rules and a priest at Oblates of St Francis De Sales, a Chaplin at Caron, told me, that you are "intellectualizing your recovery". That's a defense mechanism and it means that you have a mental disconnection with your heart and your brain. Once I completed my twenty-eight day stay at Caron, I stopped drinking.

I was still attracted to the whims of business manipulation. I went back to the hospital and they inquired, where were you? I told them that I was away on business, but some knew better. They was gossip about my shenanigans, but some wanted me to persevere with Most Health Services. I attended AA (Alcohol Anonymous) meetings and I visited Dr S., my counselor regularly. But the alcoholic in me wanted to conquer myself. There's old adage in the little book AA, twenty-four hours a day which I still read daily. The adage states that "a person can conquer himself or herself, it is better than conquering a city". That's a powerful message, but I am an obstinate person who forges ahead without caution. That's I why I became a Marine, who would charge up the hill with reckless abandon.

I stopped going to AA after ninety days. My excuse at that time was the obnoxious smoking in the AA hall and it was annoying me. I was never addicted to nicotine and my days in rehab were very unpleasant. I disliked nicotine. Yet, I loved coffee, but caffeinated coffee was never served in rehab. I was reminded by my counselors in Caron that we are all cross addicted and all mind altering substances should be removed. Of course, I told them that use of nicotine should be removed too. That's why they told me that I was "intellectualizing my addiction". That's true that I learned the hard way, but in the nineties, the addiction specialists realized that nicotine was an issue, but many alcoholics still smoke.

My final step in my recovery was that I relapsed two or three times after my rehab. I needed a spiritual awakening. I had the tools of recovery in my mind, but my soul and my heart was not in place. I spent ten days at the Jesuit Center in Wernersville, PA. It was a spiritual retreat and I prayed and cried at the Sacred Heart statue imploring my God to help me and understand myself. Once I departed from this retreat and I never drank again, one day and then another. I needed spiritual and emotional counseling and my work at Holy Redeemer was finished. I had many legal issues after that with business affairs. I was good at business but my failures outnumbered my successes. With Divine Providence, I forged ahead one day at a time, but things were not the same in business and personal relationships despite my commitment to Rita and my family. I learned over the days, months and years that my gratitude 🙏 with my family was enduring and takes time to heal the wounds. I'm still working on my journey through wellness overcoming conflict, change and conversion one day at a time.

CHAPTER 5

FIFTIES

Mid-life transition continues in my fifties, but I am clean and sober. There is a book called 'Mid Life Transition'. A **midlife** crisis is a **transition** of identity and self-confidence that can occur in middle-aged individuals, typically forty-five to sixty-four years old written by Levinson. Women and men go through mid-life crisis. It is a physical and emotional problem. Women bodies produce hormones which in turn their menses and in men are affected by all kinds of emotional issues. Separation and divorce is more common and some folks can't handle the aging process.

I learned from Caron Foundation that once you relapse, your drinking is sabotaged because your knowledge of the disease will be a detriment. That's true. I stopped drinking in April, 1987; it took upwards of three years to stabilize my emotional state. I was not interested in business, but I needed my trucking business because it paid the bills. I sold my business of Most Health Services and two custom trailers. I had to let go of some of my business connections and it was a means for my emotional unrest. We become addicted to people, places and things. I learned that lesson the hard way.

I had taken a few courses from the late eighties at Neumann University and I was still enrolled in the master's program. In the summer of 1991, I was feeling better emotionally, and I began anew taking several courses. I took two summer courses and in the fall, I took four courses and my plan was to take four more courses in the spring of 1992. I did clinical studies, professional ethics, outside supervision and marital and family counseling.

I was attending three classes per week and I began my Masters' thesis which is attached in this book. I began a practicum at Levingrin Drug and Alcohol Center for six months. I was involved in a practicum status in the master's program, but I learned a lot during that time evaluating Drug and Alcohol patients in diagnostic assessments.

I earned a Master's of Science in May 1992. I was fifty-two but I was still involved in my business and my two minority partners gave me ample time and support. I was extremely fortunate in that I had the time to complete the program.

There was an oral evaluation by three PhD's in the program and I defended my master's thesis which is included in this book. Since I was a pastoral counseling student, I combined a psychology path using a cognitive model whereby our automatic thoughts can be challenged through rational response. On the theological path, I inculcated my knowledge of Thomas Merton having read many of his books dealing with the true and false self. The director of the master's program at Neumann. Dr. V. supported and motivated me in continuing the program. At that time, he advised me in pursuing a doctorate at Loyola University.

I was ripe at that time for furthering my studies, but I decided not to pursue it because financial options were an obstacle. In my hindsight, that was a major mistake of mine because I loathed my business and I never regained any real interest. I was going through aimless motions and my business side of me was frustrated by my ambivalence in business and academics.

We had one customer who filed bankruptcy twice and we lost a deal of revenue. There was one major legal litigation against the company, me and my partners. It was a RICO civil case and it cost the company $50,000 in legal and settlement fees. It was a personal attack on my sobriety. I was white knuckling the situation. I spent a couple years in defending this legal action. Meanwhile, my nerves were in tatters. The lawsuit was settled and a federal judge looked at the case and the RICO action was unwarranted. It was a case when our minority partner never terminated his position legally at his former trucking company.

He never told me or Frank and that was the origin of the legal case. We had to pay a huge cash settlement. The monies were spent wantonly in defending the litigation. It was ludicrous case and we should have been more aggressive from inception and that case should have been settled amicably. I was never on my business game and I learned a valuable lesson, but it was too late. Besides my sobriety was on the line.

I was sober for difficult five years and I needed to talk to a psychiatrist / psychologist. I did receive anti-depressants, in the late eighties and in my late eighties. I did not tolerate them. Also, I visited Dr. B in 1988 and he greatly helped me by utilizing cognitive and behavioral skills that I learned from him. I needed an emotional boost, but it's can't be a mind altering or non-addictive drug.

I was diagnosed from Dr. B with general anxiety disorder and depression along with axis two narcissist / compulsive personality disorder. Now, I understood why I was miserable and angry. I used to drink to mask my anxieties and depression. It worsened as I aged and the business and legal problems exacerbated my issues.

I visited Dr. V, a psychiatrist who started a regiment of anti-anxiety meds like Buspar and Paxil, a SSRI (meds will be described in the book).

It look years to sort out my meds, but in summary, I ended up taking Celexa, a newer SSRI, selective serotonin reuptake inhibitor. Essentially, the synapses in an alcoholic or addicts are neurotransmitters in your brain. Dopamine and Serotonin and others are neurotransmitters - pleasure seeking chemicals in your brain. Our brain synapses are underdeveloped and the psychotropic meds fill the void. It takes time for the drug to metabolize in your body. They are not physically or psychologically addicted but the adverse effects can be devastating. Many people don't adjust well with these psychotropic medicines.

My two of my children were married in the fifties. We were blessed by their choices of spouses. Our daughter had emotional problems with an eating disorder, bulimia. It manifested when she attended college and Rita and I needed to support her. She had lost weight and she purged herself daily. Her self-image was distorted. Thank God, we found a medical doctor who specialized in eating disorders. Christine needed help and we supported her, but it was a challenge for me. My daughter is my rock, but we were distant and we didn't relate to each other. But, it changed because her doctor told me emphatically "if your daughter will get well; you need to change yourself treat her differently and accept her and love her unconditionally". That was a huge wake up for me and in short time, I changed her behavior and she and I went into weekend retreat, once again to the Jesuit center. Now, could another miracle happen with her? This was a retreat called, "Hurt, Anger and Guilt". It was a fitting name and that weekend was so uplifting. On Sunday, we wrote out in our individual paper listing our hurts, anger and guilt issues. Then we burned the paper and it was a "Letting Go and Let

God" event. Wow, it was a Eureka moment and things improved drastically and she had undergone counseling with Dr. B.

In 1998, she was married and her wonderful husband is an unconditional husband and he lets her to be herself as I learned that valuable lesson too.

Another decade in the books and the constant theme is Gratitude in Truth through Recovery, Reconciliation and Remembrance.

CHAPTER 6

SIXTIES

Wake up and smell the coffee? My favorite drink is strong coffee. But, caffeine is a drug but I can't drink too much of it because it unnerves me. It's amazing that alcoholics crave mind altering meds and it goes back to the loss of endorphins in our brains. I'm still drinking coffee and taking anti-depressants, Celexa. That's it and no other psychotropic meds. My body had adjusted to this SSRI.

My wife, Rita and I made a decision to sell our home in Horsham. We want to downsize because our family has scattered. Two are sold and two single guys are buying their own townhouses. As I stated in my fifties, I continue to work at my business albeit part time. We lost two major accounts in our warehouse and distribution business through bankruptcy and downsizing. My younger partner is maintaining the trucking side of the business and I have devoted my part time in working with recovering people. With respect to bizarre behavior, I maintain a working relationship with my psychologist, Dr. B and he had told me repeatedly that I am too impetuous and impulse control is lacking.

Yes, I'm not drinking, but my life can be chaotic. Dr. B and I talked about my heartfelt appreciation to God, but I continue to vacillate from my false self to my true self. I continue to stop myself and my anger overcomes me. It is a mood thing with me and Dr. B has exemplified DSM 1V diagnosis using dysthymia depression or possibly bi-polar 1. Emotional problems are intangible and the doctor(s) need to assess diagnostic tests and look at behavioral criteria. Depression is biological or reactive and DNA blood tests can be done to pinpoint DNA markers. I'm impatient with myself and others. I continue to remind myself that I need to count to ten instead flying off the handle.

I did see another psychiatrist in my early sixties and he couldn't diagnose my bi-polar symptoms. He corroborated the diagnosis of dysthymia or mild depression. He did prescribe lithium and / or Depakote. I am, also, an obsessive -compulsive person which Dr. B observed in therapy. I was counting numbers like one, two or three and repeated the sequences. I would turn on / off lights, hence, my mind would go into circles. The OCD issue was a major factor in adolescence. I saw doctor then and he did not prescribe any medication. Although, he suggested a behavioral cue, once the obsessive thought came into my mind, I needed to tell myself that it is an irrational fear and my thoughts cannot change anything. Distract yourself intentionally during the in the obsessive thought and the compulsive act will dissipate. That behavioral modification in my OCD worked for me. It was not a panacea, but neurotic thoughts and actions did not escalate.

It's a chronic anxiety and depression issue with me. I decided not to follow- up with any more psychotropic medicine. I have experimented with 10-15 non-addicted meds over the 15 year span from my recovery. After the recent behavioral lapses and my containing counseling with Dr. B, I accepted myself and I made up my mind to live one day at a time. My progressive cognitive therapy with Dr. B continued and the combination of counseling and only one medicine, Celexa has worked for me. It has helped my anxiety and depression issues.

In the early sixties, I retired from my business and it was my time to Let Go and Let God. Divine Providence was my savior. The last five years was a torturing time and my anger intensified. I had to extricate myself definitely from the business and an early retirement was providential. "C 'est la Vie" - such is life and thank God.

Now, in mid-sixties, Rita and I sold our primary home and we bought a smaller single home, over age fifty community. We moved into this furnished sample home and my tethered chains to my former business were severed. I was in peace by removing myself from the grief associated with business.

I give 100% grateful appreciation to Rita, my wife who stood steadfastly with me amidst my emotional problems. My counselors like Dr. B and Fr. M offered me faith, hope and love and that gave me serenity.

My serenity prayer is attached and, in fact, the new Pastor in our new parish suggested that I can begin a weekly Serenity group in our church. I advertised this Serenity program and in the first week, ten people attended - mostly women. My plan was to utilize a book called "Serenity". It was a compilation of the twelve steps using the AA model and associated biblical passages. I was the leader of the group and we took turns reciting AA steps and biblical prayers. Members of the group were challenged by alcohol and drug family issues. I used the cognitive model of psychology as my underlying theme. This went on twelve weeks citing the twelve AA steps. We lost a couple members in the group but the Pastor liked the program and the feedback from the group was very good. I really enjoyed my part and interacting with the group. I was connected to something special and spiritual. It was meaningful and it humbled me.

We started another two part session, but we didn't have much attendance. A small group should be comprised of five to ten people and the second session was comprised five or less. Three or two left and we were down to one or two. We concluded the twelve steps for another three months. The Pastor asked me to join the Parish Council and he, also, asked me to do individual counseling in the parish. I was not interested in charging a counseling fee because it was my goal is to support others, and to help the church. I had a wonderful rapport with the pastor and he was generous and gracious. Things didn't work for me in that parish council and interactions with people were generally good, but I wanted to be the leader. This goes back to my old days when I wanted to be the 'boss'. Sure, I always listened to others, but the ultimate decision was mine. Yes, I matured in recovery but my stinking thinking gets hold of me. At that time,

I was involved with the property management in our local community. There were 400 homes in that specific community. I volunteered my services awhile back since I lived next to a pond. There were many geese located there and I got involved in this property management in order to eliminate the geese. I worked with the county wildlife department and we all did a good job by roiling the geese eggs, posting - no feed signs and using no lethal banger pistols. I was working with the local community and I'm working with my catholic parish and Rita are attending Mass two to three times a week.

Things were good for few years! I'm not seeing Dr. B, but I am working with him professionally because I refer some of my counseling clients to see him. Now, the community group asked me to be the Chairman of the property committee. There were upwards of fifteen volunteers like me to attend bi-monthly meetings.

In my late sixties, I got involved with them and it was very chaotic and shades of my past. My responsibility was to maintain the full and complete property working with the sub-contractors, the community board of directors and the management association.

I had to coordinate with landscaping and snow removal contractors. It was early and mild winter in 2007.

But, in March we had several inches of snow came down. We had a three inch rule; if the snow accumulated over three inches, we would call up the contractor. I didn't call up the contractor because where I was located we had under three inches and my committee people agreed with me. Well, things came apart quickly and remember we had 800 people in that community. They don't want to pay more community fees than possible, but they, also want their cake and to eat it too. The community people took their angst with me and the volunteers like me knew better, but they unfairly sided with the community.

In summary with the sixties, my reaction with the aforementioned was arbitrary and capricious. I regressed to my earlier self of control and anger. I quit my position in the community and I couldn't handle the heat or better said, I could handle the cold and I became a persona non grata. Everything went down the hill and it was a cold tundra and I wanted to depart living in this community. There were other things going on negatively in that community and my affiliation with counseling in the church was strained. One of the things that, simultaneously with my community and the church, that one of the people that I was doing family and marital counseling became belligerent.

The woman wanted me to testify against her husband stated that he was an alcoholic. I believe that he was not an alcoholic. I told her in uncertain terms. It was a vindictive act against me, her spouse, and our church. It turned out that she was fallacious in her quest for reconciliation and she wanted to blame and censure him. Once I remind that I was a volunteer in the church and I had no interest in getting into legal and spousal matters. I had a meeting with the pastor in the rectory and she was in another room.

I knew that I was going to move away and I told the pastor that I appreciated him as a person and my pastor. I will not be counseling anymore in the parish, subsequently, then I had spoken to the disgruntled woman that I will not be testifying for her in court. I didn't agree with her and I suggested that she should speak directly with the pastor now and in the future.

That's another decade of mixed emotions, as I reflect on the merits and detriments of this age. Thank God, I am still not drinking and I have given myself in charitable ways. I have not handled things purposefully, but my erratic temperament is cause for concern. I am introspective and my seventies will await us.

CHAPTER 7

SEVENTIES

Rita and I moved from the community association and it took a year or two given that we were in the throes of national economic meltdown and housing prices slumped. It was another Godsend in that I didn't do well in that community association. We decided to move to our summer condo in Ocean City, New Jersey and put our furniture in storage.

I was seventy-one and our plan was to relax with no counseling and no interaction on outside interests. Rita has been involved in church affairs, particularly, in music. She was self-taught in guitar and she loves to sing. Initially, her plan was to get involved with the parish choir. I, myself was discerning God's Will again. I'm always determined to seek God's Will, but my will gets compromised by other things like personal determination. Then outside relationships complicate the status quo.

Rita is a blessed person. She doesn't get into personal issues and she follows the rules and regulations. She is a trusting and unconditional soul. Within a year of our time in Ocean City, she volunteered for a food cupboard organizing food distribution in the local area. It was only a monthly commitment but, she is so prudent in determining her abilities. Once, she commits to something unlike me, she has exceptional forbearance. The manager of the cupboard asked Rita; if her husband wanted to drive my car delivering bags of food to the needy. Of course, I wouldn't say no! I accompanied her in the next month. It was easy in that I loaded grocery bags and I delivered to five to seven local indigent people. I was automatically caught up into talking and praying with them. That's my forte! Maybe, it was the next month or so, I was delivering routinely to the same people.

One of the elder women in my route asked me to take her to the local phone store. She stated that her phone service would have been stopped that day. I was finished in delivering the bags of food and I knew I had the time and it was ten minutes away.

Well, I took her to the utility store and she didn't have enough money. Without any hesitation, I didn't have any cash and I told her that I needed to get cash from my wife. That's was my undoing. I only needed twenty dollars and it was ten minutes away. I went back to the cupboard in order to borrow the money to Rita. I was in a hurry, apparently, the manager saw me and asked her, where is Phil going? Rita is an extremely honest person and she told the woman what I was doing. I took twenty dollars to the store, paid the utility bill and took the elderly woman back to her apartment.

I then picked up Rita and we went on our merry way. Rita suggested to me that rules were broken at the cupboard, but no elaboration. The following month and my last month too as it turned out, the manager who was a very personable suggested in a nice way that you can't drive the outreach people. Of course, I'm ready for a retort, but in a nice way, we agreed and proceeded in delivering the food packages to the destitute. The last delivery was the elderly woman who was crying and emotional. I know people and she seem to be manipulative, albeit sincere. She told me that she had terminal cancer. She couldn't drive and then she asked me to drive to Cape May for a legal hearing. I answered to her I can't drive because it was the cupboard's rules. She pleaded to me about driving her in a different day and asked me for my cell number.

Consequently, she called me a couple times and finally, I called her back and I couldn't drive her. I was ambivalent because I can't get mixed up with driving around her and there are social services do that and the food cupboard manager told Rita that this woman might have cheated in them that she was not giving her proof of income in order to get free food. I summed up my final position and I didn't want to get involved with any of them including my charitable services to the cupboard. It was another painstaking encounter with me by ignoring the regulations, by trying to help someone in distress and ultimately, I got loss in the process.

After eight years still living in Ocean City, we had innumerable examples to buy in OCNJ and PA. I have become very gun-shy and I can't make big business decisions anymore. I don't do any volunteering anymore. I write blogs using a pseudonym, Truthseeker and it's easy to avoid outside relational situations. I remain open to my family and I spend great time introspection of myself and my continuing relationship with my wife and my family. Rita continues to do her thing, singing in the choir, attending church prayer groups and volunteering in the food cupboard.

In 2015, Rita and I celebrated our fiftieth wedding anniversary in April and March, I turned seventy-five. In May of that year, I had a moderate stroke. I don't party anymore for over thirty years and I can't use that as an excuse. This stroke was surreal for me. I went to bed late and I awoke late. I went into the bathroom then I fell on the floor but I was semiconscious. But, I couldn't speak.

The following is fortuitous: A nurse was awaiting for me to check my vital signs for a life insurance policy. Rita heard the noise and she saw me lying on the bathroom floor. She then asked the nurse to look at me. The nurse, intuitively, stated to Rita that I might have had a stroke and called 911. Within ten minutes the crew observed that I needed real help and they rushed me to the local hospital in Somers Point. I was still in a bewildering state of semiconscious. I heard the sights and sounds, but they were administering IV - Alteplase can be given to patients with cervical artery dissection, seizure at onset and evidence of acute ischemia on the brain. That saved my life and I was in the hospital for five days undergoing tests. They diagnosed me with an ischemic stroke, non-hemorrhagic. But I could speak a little and I couldn't identify basic words like toothbrush, comb and certain people. I was diagnosed with Aphasia is a communication disorder that results from damage or injury to language parts of the brain. It's more common in older adults, particularly those who have had a stroke.

"Aphasia gets in the way of a person's ability to use or understand words. Aphasia does not impair the person's intelligence. People who have aphasia may have difficulty speaking and finding the "right" words to complete their thoughts. They may also have problems understanding conversation, reading and comprehending written words, writing words, and using numbers." The part of the brain was affected by my stroke in the Broca's area or the Broca area is a region in the frontal lobe of the dominant hemisphere, usually the left, of the brain with functions linked to speech.

After my release from the hospital, I followed to with a speech pathologist weekly for months. I slowly regained my speech, maybe, seventy-five percent. After four months, I plateaued in my speech. Given my advanced age, the pathways in the brain can be rerouted but it takes time. I was so fortunate that I had no physical limitations, no impediments in hearing or understanding words. I continue to meet with a neurologist once a year and he gives me annual vascular tests. The stroke was caused by a genetic predisposition to high blood lipids and now I take Plavix, daily for blood thinning along with high-dosages anti-cholesterol medication. I can't recite stories since I can't find certain words, but I can read and write. That's my life at 2018 and looking forward for age seventy-nine on 3/28. I'm writing about my life and in my Epilogue, I will review my life's pros and cons. I will comment and contemplate on my life and give 100 to my Maker, Divine Providence. Without Him, I would be alone or dead, derelict in spirit and unconditionally grateful to my wife, Rita and my family who has given me perseverance.

If you detect syntax or grammar issues, blame me because I did not do professional editing; it's my way of Letting Go and Letting God do His Thing in my life. I not interested in selling books. I'm only interested in genuinely helping others by reaching out to you.

EPILOGUE

What is the meaning of life? After seventy-nine years of life, I have an idea what is the meaning of life and my biography reflects Aristotle a great philosopher who wrote about happiness:

"Happiness is the meaning and the purpose of life, the whole aim and end of human existence."

One of my wonderful alcoholic counselors, Dr S. said to me prior to my entrance in my twenty-eight day rehabilitation. He stated that you have no meaning in your life and it is disguised by your false self and your alcoholism. Once you cooperate with trained specialists, you will understand what your meaning is in your life. You have been living in a bad dream and God has given you an opportunity to open up your eyes and embrace His Divine Blessings. Dr S. was a trained psychologist and a Christian minister. Dr. S. died a year from cancer after my first year of recovery and his message has been resonated in me through all of my days in recovery.

My life has been embolden by the blessings from my Good Lord. I am a human full of good and bad traits. It takes a while to understand the spiritual side of your life. I was reared in a Roman Catholic family and parents were good people. They strove to understand the zenith and the nadir of their lives. Once I corresponded to God's good graces then I understood their struggles with alcohol and codependency. My mother was a codependent (enabler) and my father was an alcoholic (counter dependent). They were attracted to each other's failings. They loved each other, but the disease of alcohol obliterated real meaning in their lives.

I'm convinced that we are instilled by our Maker for a goal to achieve. When we look at young people, middle age and old people, we all strive through prayer to discern God's Will.

My conjecture is that we have a purpose in life. Once the purpose is achieved, God calls us back to Him. It could be a major accomplishment in one's life like finding a Cure in a disease or a minor achievement like a Cause and Effect of a baby's birth and death. That's why abortion is a terrible evil. An abortion interferes in God's moral and natural law. Life is a meaningful event and that's why we strive to overcome our obstacles because the struggles are pathways to eternal salvation. Don't give up!

God knows in His infinite wisdom, that we are human and we are inter-connected with a form or another. I am convinced that all prayers and acts of charity towards others will never be forgotten by God. Everything that is been done by us - good or bad - is recorded in the book of life. Everything that we do for others is another notch in our belt to envelop our true selves. Everything that we do for God by overcoming our false selves, we achieve spiritual conversion and ultimate perfection. That's our meaning in life.

As I reflect on my foibles in my aforementioned life's story, I'm reminded that these shortcomings in my personality or temperament were ongoing tests of character and courage. My way is finitely different than God's infinite way. Character is built through adversity and courage and it's developed by taking one step and another step until your steps are immobile.

The Serenity Prayer is my inspiration:

Acceptance of things that we cannot change. Courage to makes changes in your life that we can understand. Wisdom is to know the difference. us

SECTION II

INTRODUCTION TO DRUGS AND KNOWLEDGE OF THEM

Opioids are a class of drugs naturally found in the opium poppy plant. Some prescription opioids are made from the plant directly, and others are made by scientists in labs using the same chemical structure. Opioids are often used as medicines because they contain chemicals that relax the body and can relieve pain. Prescription opioids are used mostly to treat moderate to severe pain, though some opioids can be used to treat coughing and diarrhea. Opioids can also make people feel very relaxed and "high" - which is why they are sometimes used for non-medical reasons. This can be dangerous because opioids can be highly addictive, and overdoses and death are common. Heroin is one of the world's most dangerous opioids, and is never used as a medicine in the United States.

Fentanyl is a synthetic opioid that is eighty times stronger than morphine. Pharmaceutical fentanyl was developed for pain management treatment of cancer patients, applied in a patch on the skin. Because of its powerful opioid properties, Fentanyl is added to heroin to increase its potency and it is paramount in drug street use. Prescription opioids used for pain relief are generally safe when taken for a short time and as prescribed by a doctor, but they can be abused.

https://www.dea.gov/factsheets/fentanyl

If you suspect someone has overdosed, the most important step to take is to call 911 so he or she can receive immediate medical attention. Once medical personnel arrive, they will administer naloxone / narcan. Naloxone is a medicine that can treat an opioid overdose when given right away. It works by rapidly binding to opioid receptors in the brain.

When most people think of physical addiction, they are usually attributing it to the thought of the physical withdrawal symptoms that occur when someone stops giving their body the substance they have been using regularly. Once a person begins using on a daily or regular basis, the body becomes dependent on that drug. This means the cells can't function properly. As a result, painful withdrawal symptoms like nausea and tremors occur which causes many people to reach for their drug of choice to alleviate the pain.

The psychological side of addiction represents the compulsion of the mind to drink or use drugs. This side of addiction can occur even if the person doesn't display physical dependency symptoms. Psychological addiction is when a person is emotionally connected to a drug or alcohol based on their need. It is common for people who use drugs or alcohol that may not cause severe withdrawal symptoms. However, their psychological state creates an extreme desire for drugs that can result negatively in many ways causing loss of sleep, anxiety, depression, and changes in appetite.

DrugAbuse.gov offers an insightful explanation based on brain image studies from people addicted to drugs. The study found, physical changes in areas of the brain that are critical for judgment, decision making, learning, memory, and behavior control in addicted people. The main difference between alcoholism and drug addiction is that alcohol is legal and many controlled drugs are not. We also live in a culture where drinking alcohol is sociably acceptable.

Alcohol and drugs create euphoria in the brain which results by the release of dopamine and serotonin, brain neurotransmitters. When addiction occurs, the brain adapts to the substance and it no longer has the same effect, but there is a biological effect of withdrawal. Much of the reasons why some people develop an addiction are unknown. However, the main danger lies in the reasons behind the use of a substance. Those who use drug or alcohol as a coping mechanism like stress or depression. They evolve negatively by repetitive usage and their brains become less responsive to the positive effects. This is true for alcohol & drugs.

Many people enter alcohol or drug rehab thinking that once they are clean of one substance, they can use other drugs. It's called cross addiction. Therefore, some people will stop taking illegal drugs and drink alcohol instead. However, the psychological behind the addiction are often suppressed or repressed by users.

TOTAL ABSTINENCE IS RECOMMENDED FOR TRUE RECOVERY.

10 Facts about Marijuana That Will Change Your Mind by TFP Student Action. https://www.tfpstudentaction.org https://www.tfpstudentaction.org/blog/facts-about-marijuana-that-you-should-know

SECTION III

A JOURNEY TOWARD WHOLENESS THROUGH A PROCESS OF CONFLICT * CHANGE * CONVERSION

Philip J. Klauder, Jr.
DATE OF ENTRY: SEPTEMBER 4, 1985

DATE OF EXPECTED GRADUATION: MA Y 16, 1992

A PAPER SUBMITTED TO THE PASTORAL COUNSELING PROGRAM OF NEUMANN COLLEGE, A STON, PENNSYLVANIA, FOR THE MASTER OF SCIENCE DEGREE.

INTRODUCTION:

This integration paper is entitled a journey toward wholeness given the clinical and theological approaches that I have chosen; namely, cognitive therapy for my clinical style and Merton's theology of the true and false self. One metaphor for wholeness could be the music of a finely tuned symphony with each instrument guided by the maestro in order to produce an exquisite sound. This is order and balance of the first degree. Wholeness is the exact opposite of chaos. Wholeness gives meaning to truth and life. We are burdened by illusory things as Merton talks about in my theological section and negative or automatic dysfunctional thoughts as Beck discusses in my clinical section which impairs our movement toward wholeness.

The sounds of solitude and serenity can be achieved if we listen attentively to our inner voice; not distracted by the confusion of noise and pretentious sounds of our world. We are on a journey inward to listen for meaning and messages of truth that can be bought to light. The inner freedom, the Gospel promises is only understood when our identity in Christ is nourished. It is experienced when our inner lives are in syncopation with our ability to hear and respond to the rhythms that the Spirit offers in calling us out of ourselves. The journey in Christ is replete with suffering but rewarded with eternal salvation.

MY CLINICAL APPROACH

Primary Therapeutic Approach to Treatment:
Cognitive therapy as defined by Aaron T. Beck M.D. is an active, directive, time-limited, structured approach used to treat a variety of psychiatric disorders;

for example, depression, anxiety, phobias and personality disorders (Beck, 1990, p.5).

The underlying theoretical rationale of cognitive therapy states that an individual's affect and behavior are largely determined by the way in which he or she structures the world (Beck, 1976, p.216). Cognitions are verbal or pictorial events in one's stream of consciousness. These cognitions are based on attitudes or assumptions (schemas) developed from previous experiences. For example, if a person interprets all of his/her experiences in terms of whether he/she is competent and adequate, his/her thinking can be dominated by the schema: "Unless I do everything perfectly, I am a failure." Consequently, he/she reacts to situations in terms of adequacy even when they are unrelated to competency.

The specific therapeutic techniques employed are utilized within the framework. Of the cognitive model of psychopathology. The therapeutic techniques are designed to identify, reality-test, and correct dysfunctional beliefs or schemas underlying these cognitions. The cognitive therapist helps the patient to think and act more realistically and adaptively about his psychological problems. A variety of cognitive and behavioral strategies are utilized in cognitive therapy. This approach consists of highly specific learning experiences designed to teach the client the following guidelines which are recorded by the client on a Daily Record of Dysfunctional Thoughts (Burns, FEELING GOOD 1980, p.62).

[1] To monitor the client's negative and automatic thoughts.

[2] To recognize the connections between cognition, affect and behavior.

[3] To examine the evidence for and against the automatic thought.

[4] To substitute more reality-oriented interpretations for these biased cognitions.

[5] Learn to identify and thereby altering the dysfunctional beliefs which distort ones' experiences.

In contrast to psychoanalytic therapy, the content of cognitive therapy is focused on "here-and-now" problems and little attention is paid to childhood recollections except to clarify present observations. Cognitive therapy contrasts with behavioral therapy in it is greater emphasis on the client's internal or mental experiences such as thoughts, feelings and attitudes. The overall strategy of cognitive therapy differs from other modalities by emphasizing the empirical investigation from the clients' automatic thoughts, inferences, conclusions and assumptions. Therapy generally consists of fifteen to twenty-five sessions at weekly intervals culminating in a few bi-weekly sessions for closure. There are three or four booster sessions in the year following termination for support.

Clinical Assumptions about the Human Person:

Every individual, as a result of his/her personal cumulative and conditioned learning experiences, acquires and stores a separate and unique subjective thought system (Bailey, 1990, p.30). This thought system becomes the eye through which that individual sees the world. People create their own thoughts through internalization which, in turn, shape their perceptions, feelings and behaviors. Since each person's thought system is unique then we experience things differently. We have our own separate reality and when we abuse or misunderstand this separate reality then conflicts and negativity result.

Some other clinical assumptions about the human person are our fluctuations in and out of different states of minds or moods which are actually levels of psychological functioning. In low moods our level of functioning is reduced and we feel insecure, anxious and impatient sometimes unable to concentrate. Conversely, high connection between our thoughts and what we are experiencing in our states of mind or high moods are optimal levels of mental functioning. In these pleasant states, people naturally have self-esteem and feelings of well-being that do not depend on immediate circumstances or external stimuli. Interest, motivation and achievement are high. In higher moods our psychological functioning is better and we realize that our thoughts affect what we experience. Feelings and emotions are indicators of a person's immediate state of mind or psychological functioning.

Positive feelings indicate a state of mental health, serenity and order. Negative feelings indicate a state of mental disorder, fear and chaos. A person's change of heart is affected through awareness, not denial, through balance, not ridgity, through commitment not confusion, through determination not doom or ennui - one step at a time.

Ethical Assumptions in the Pastoral Counseling Relationship:

A commitment to confidentiality lies at the very core of psychotherapy. Within the pastoral counseling relationship the client is called upon to discuss in a candid and frank way all manner of socially unacceptable instincts and urges, immature and perverse sexual thoughts and deeds. To speak of such things to another human being requires an atmosphere of impeccable trust and confidence. The very needs of any helping profession require that confidentiality exist and be enforced.

Confidentiality is a quality of private information that is divulged with the implicit or explicit promise and the reasonable expectation that it will not be further disclosed except for the purpose for which it was provided (Stromberg, 1988, p.371).

The problems associated with a client's self-determination and confidentiality are diverse and they create challenging responses to the personal responsibility of the counselor. First and foremost, if one is to handle such dilemmas skillfully and be fair and open to all parties, then an understanding of the legal and ethical concepts is mandated.

Otherwise, the counselor can overlook potential problems, or rely on supposed legal protections which do not exist. Our responsibility is do what is right and operate under strict legal and ethical standards while manifesting genuine and unconditional care and support for our clients.

MY THEOLOGICAL APPROACH TO PASTORAL COUNSELING

Primary Theological Method for Integration:

The inspiration underlying my own spiritual integration follows the work of Thomas Merton and the question of one's ultimate human identity. Merton's message is that we are one with God. Merton explains that the self that begins the journey to God is not the self that arrives. According to Merton who writes: "Every one of us is shadowed by an illusory person: a false self' (Mc Donnell, 1985, p. 68). It is this self that dies along the way until there is no one left but our true self who becomes our whole self before our God. The death of the false self and the resurrection of the true self embodies bringing our entire life into a transforming, loving communion with our Maker. A prayerful pursuit of Merton's understanding the true self can bring us to a fuller realization of our own ultimate identity being one with God in Christ. Merton does not question the reality of the empirical self

Furthermore, in the spiritual life a deep respect must be accorded to our whole person, including the mundane realities of day by day experiences and the self that evolves from these conflicts. Merton is understood to say that when the relative identity of the ego is taken to be one's only identity and we become the center around our existence then our empirical identity becomes our false self. This false self becomes an obstacle to realizing our true self.

The foundation of the false self and true self as concepts that Merton coined is not a novel spirituality but rather a synthesis of scripture and tradition. In Genesis we see that the foundation of our life and identity resides in our relationship with God and the consequential spiritual death that occurred when Adam and Eve disobeyed their Creator. From earliest times there was hope for deliverance from this self-inflicted bondage to death. Israel yearned for a Messiah and her pleas were answered in the person of Jesus, our Redeemer. By Jesus' acceptance of the Father's Will he has restored our relationship with God. Jesus, the New Adam, takes the effects of Adam's disobedience upon himself and in his death "death dies". The tendency to sin and death is a mystery. It is the darkness that has been redeemed by Christ but which we must constantly struggle and daily carry our cross. Merton calls this tendency to sin our "false self" (Finley, 1985, pgs.23-35).

Merton discovered true communion with others in his solitude and that was his vocation. The vocation of people in the world is to find solitude in the midst of others. The true self embraces both solitude and others. The false-self rejects both solitude and others. "The way to find the real world is not merely to measure and observe what is outside us but to discover our own inner ground. For that is where the world is, first of all in my deepest self" (Merton, 1971, p154).

For Merton, the all-encompassing tenets of certain social standards such as power, success and wealth must be transcended; if we are to be free and able to love and be available to each other in spirit and in truth.

This principle of Christian solitude is for Merton necessary for a created person to maintain his or her integrity and wholeness. Merton tells us that in seeking realization of our true self in prayer. We should not look for a method but cultivate an attitude of faith, openness and in trust. Faith is the bond that unites us to Him in the Spirit who gives us light and love (Merton, 1971, p.34). The emphasis is on faith. Faith itself is a gift of the Spirit given to us in Christ. The ultimate self, the true self in God finds clarity only by faith. Our death and resurrection will dispel the illusory shadow of doubt and possible despair. In faith we are presented with an obscure vision of the mystery of our own deepest self-made one with God through Christ. The obscure promise of faith is the source of hope which itself is a gift of God. Hope is the death of despair and the root of our faith. Faith and hope are themselves fulfilled only in love.

As Saint Paul expresses it, "There are in the end three things that last: faith, hope and love. The greatest of these is love" (1 Cot. 13:13). Love is the energy of life and the power toward wholeness. Love is the ultimate consummation of the true self. Love endures all things and since love never ends, GOD is LOVE.

Theological View of the Human Person:

Pope Kyril I, a prototype of Pope John XXIII writes in a private journal:

"Yesterday I met a whole man. It is a rare experience, but always an illuminating one. It costs so much to be a full human being that there are very few who have the enlightenment, or the courage, to pay the price... One has to abandon altogether the search for security, and reach out to the risk of living with full arms. One has to embrace the world like a lover, and yet demand no easy return for love. One has to accept pain as a condition of existence. One has to court doubt and darkness as the cost of knowing. One needs a will stubborn in conflict, but apt to the total consequence of living and dying" (West, 1963, pg.254). What a magnificent characterization of our humanness as we struggle toward wholeness! The search for wholeness in my Christian perspective is very much a part of our journey in Christ. When psychologist Carl Jung spoke of wholeness as the fundamental movement toward growth in the human personality and individuation, he provided a balance between psychology and spirituality. An understanding of human growth invites us to participate in a process of full collaboration with the Divine Spirit in a universal movement directed to the fulfillment of our humanity. Whether we espouse the Jungian philosophy of Self, the Patristic notion of the Heart, the Pauline principle of the Inner-Man or

Jesus Christ's centering view of the Child, the ultimate search for all of us is meaning and a movement toward the divine. The process of going deeper within through the suffering of the soul is a pathway to wholeness. The resolution of our inner conflict between the true self and false self that prevents us from owning our self-worth is made possible by claiming the gift of faith. We, thereby, enter into a relationship with our Christ through our worth and salvation is assured. Wholeness has to do with our freedom from inner fear. Through self-knowledge and discovery we consciously see our conflicts. Through self-acceptance and determination we make our choices. Through self-forgiveness and surrender we then reconcile ourselves with our Creator. Wholeness, when open to the Spirit of God, is the seedbed for holiness (Fenhagen, 1985, p.9).

The Christian life involves more than growth and development. It involves conversion and transformation, a movement toward the God who created us and who continues to sustain us. Christian faith is about an inner transformation of consciousness; a metanoia, in which the Apostle Paul says, "put on the mind of Christ in the Spirit and live a life of Christ in the Spirit". I have been crucified with Christ, it is no longer I who live, but

Christ who lives in me" (Gal.2:20). "When anyone is united to Christ, there is a new world: the old order has gone, and a new order has already begun" (2 Cor.5:17). The pastoral mission of the Church is to develop men and women who can walk with one another amidst hurt and separations we struggle through suffering and healing to find wholeness in our lives. But it is, also, the development of holiness while working through our experiences of brokenness and wholeness in which we nourish the gift of faith.

Faith opens to us the mystery of God's magnanimous benevolence. Faith draws us into worlds other than our own. Faith invites us to witness that dimension of reality that is just beyond our sight; not blinded in fear, but alive with a clear vision of our quest for wholeness and holiness

Ethical Assumptions in the Pastoral Counseling Relationship:

A commitment to confidentiality lies at the very core of psychotherapy. Within the pastoral counseling relationship the client is called upon to discuss in a candid and frank way all manner of socially unacceptable instincts and urges, immature and perverse sexual thoughts and deeds. To speak of such things to another human being requires an atmosphere of impeccable trust and confidence. The very needs of any helping profession require that confidentiality exist and be enforced. Confidentiality is a quality of private information that is divulged with the implicit or explicit promise and the reasonable expectation that it will not be further disclosed except for the purpose for which it was provided (Stromberg, 1988, p.371).

The problems associated with a client's self-determination and confidentiality are diverse and they create challenging responses to the personal responsibility of the counselor. First and foremost, if one is to handle such dilemmas skillfully and be fair to all parties, then an understanding of the legal and ethical concepts is mandated. Otherwise, the counselor can overlook potential problems, or rely on supposed legal protections which do not exist. Our responsibility is do what is right and operate under strict legal and ethical standards while manifesting genuine and unconditional care for all clients.

In contrast to psychoanalytic therapy, the content of cognitive therapy is focused on "here-and-now" problems and little attention is paid to childhood recollections except to clarify present observations. Cognitive therapy contrasts with behavioral therapy and has a greater emphasis on the clients' internal or mental experiences such as thoughts, feelings and attitudes. The overall strategy of cognitive therapy differs from other modalities by emphasizing the empirical investigation of the client's automatic thoughts, inferences, conclusions and assumptions. Therapy generally consists of fifteen to twenty-five sessions at weekly intervals culminating in a few bi-weekly sessions for closure. There are three or four booster sessions in the year following termination for support.

Clinical Assumptions about the Human Person:

Every individual, as a result of his/her personal cumulative and conditioned learning experiences, acquires and stores a separate and unique subjective thought system (Bailey, 1990, p.30). This thought system becomes the eye in which that individual sees the world. People create their own thoughts through internalization which, in turn, shape their perceptions, feelings and behaviors. Since each person's thought system is unique then we experience things differently. We have our own separate reality and when we abuse or misunderstand this separate reality then conflicts and negativity result.

Some other clinical assumptions about the human person are our fluctuations in and out of different states of minds or moods which are actually levels of psychological functioning. In low moods our level of functioning is reduced and we feel insecure, anxious and impatient sometimes unable to concentrate. There is a high connection between our thoughts and what we are experiencing in states of mind or high moods are optimal levels of mental functioning. In these pleasant states, people naturally have self-esteem and feelings of well-being that do-not depend on immediate circumstances or external stimuli. Interest, motivation and achievement are high. In higher moods our psychological functioning is better and we realize that our thoughts affect what we experience. Feelings and emotions are indicators of a person's immediate state of mind or psychological functioning.

Positive feelings indicate a state of mental health, serenity and order. Negative feelings indicate a state of mental disorder, fear and chaos. A person's change of heart is comes from awareness, not denial, through balance, not ridgity, through commitment, not confusion, through determination not doom or ennui - one step at a time.

Ethical Assumptions in the Pastoral Counseling Relationship:

A commitment to confidentiality lies at the very core of psychotherapy. Within the pastoral counseling relationship the client is called upon to discuss in a candid and frank way all manner of socially unacceptable instincts and urges, immature and perverse sexual thoughts and deeds. To speak of such things to another human being requires an atmosphere of impeccable trust and confidence. The very needs of any helping profession require that confidentiality exist and be enforced.

Confidentiality is a quality of private information that is divulged with the implicit or explicit promise and the reasonable expectation that it will not be further disclosed except for the purpose for which it was provided (Stromberg, 1988, p.371). The problems associated with a client's self-determination and confidentiality are diverse and they create challenging responses to the personal responsibility of the counselor. First and foremost; if one is to handle such dilemmas skillfully and be fair to all parties, then an understanding of the legal and ethical concepts is mandated. Otherwise, the counselor can overlook potential problems, or rely on supposed legal protections which do not exist. Our responsibility is do what is right and operate under strict legal and ethical standards while manifesting genuine and unconditional care for all.

CASE PRESENTATION

1. Demographics: Robert L. is a 15 year old white male. His parents who are both employed have been presently separated for about a year. They come from a suburban, middle class neighborhood. Robert is Roman Catholic and has one younger brother, age 12.

2. Initial Clinical Observations: The client is a short, lean, enthusiastic young man who manifests a radiant smile with a deceptive charm. His dress is school attire. The client is a courteous, cooperative, reticent young man whose speech is lucid.

3. Primary Presenting Problem: I have seen the client weekly since January, 1992 for adjustment-problems that he has associated with his mother's abusive drinking. He was referred by my supervisor and principal of Archbishop Wood High School, Fr. C.M. The mother's drinking had intensified over

the past few months and she has been in and out of detoxification centers. The client has been emotionally abused but he cannot identify any emotions other than frustration. He has sought guidance and support from church and school counselors.

4. Personal /Social History: The client has been living in an alcoholic environment for some time. He has assumed much of the responsibility in the home since his father left a year ago because of the wife's alcoholic behavior. The younger brother seems to be apathetic to the whole process. The paternal grandparents who live on the same block have given some degree of balance and order to the deteriorating situation. The father recently was awarded custody and the two boys now live with the paternal grandparents. My client is glad to be out of the alcoholic home. He resists some of the control and discipline he now experiences with his grandparents and this has caused additional frustration. The client's social support network consist of a select few friends, male and female, his paternal grandparents, and school and church counselors. The relationship with the father is tenuous.

5. Mental Status: The client is frustrated and confused about his feelings. He has internalized much anger and resentment toward his mother and, also, his father especially for leaving them. He has witnessed a great deal of alcohol abuse and has been let down repeatedly by his mothers' relapses. He has latent depressive and anxiety symptoms but hides them well given his coping skills. Once he animatedly articulates what he perceives is a crisis he then relaxes and goes about his business without really getting in touch with his true feelings. His memory is good but his insight and judgment are poor. There is no active neurotic or psychotic symptomology.

6. Medical History: The client although frail is healthy and speaks of no medical problems. He claims that he has a hearing impairment but I have not observed a problem. He has not seen a medical professional and he is not taking any medication.

7. Psychodynamic Formulation: The client's defense mechanisms of denial and repression of anger and hurt are evidenced in the verbatim where I confront him about his feelings (342P). Rob, exclaims: "I don't know. Well, it really does not bother me anymore. I

don't know why. It just can't because (pause) nothing has changed. It hurts because I know she is still drinking and one more day she is not (off it)" (p.10, 1.345C). Because of the desertion of the father from the home and the mother's alcoholic behavior, my client has reversed roles in the family process. His parentification with regard to family responsibility has given him more control and latitude than he emotionally can handle. Therefore, his school grades have dropped and he is doing his thing which amounts to repressing his ambivalent feelings about his parents. He is unsure and confused about his true feelings. He is unable to express anger about his mother's alcoholic behavior and his father's separation.

DSM IIIR. Diagnosis, Prognosis, and Overview of Treatment.

Psychosocial stressors: separation of father from the home.

Severity: 5 - Severe. An additional Axis I

Separation anxiety disorder for adolescents is considered but not an indicator lack of active symptoms.

The client's mother is presently in an alcohol rehabilitation center and the client is experiencing social contact with his father and his school grades have been gradually improving. By employing cognitive therapy and role playing I am attempting to get the client to understand about the role of his mixed feelings and to accept them as a natural process of growth and development. Rob has a strong ego and superego which will help him with the conviction and motivation necessary to develop once he understands: that as a hero-child or family caretaker. He has not been taking care of himself. He has assumed more responsibility than his diminutive shoulders can hold. The client has resisted going to Alateen for support, but I am working on a contact with him for that purpose.

The prognosis is favorable but much has to do with his acceptance of himself as a unique young person with co-dependent traits. He cannot control his mother's behavior but he can help her by maintaining his own autonomy and personal emotional identity.

The death of the false self-associated with the insidious nature of alcoholism upon the family is given to the resurrection of the true self. When my client endures conflict and suffering for growth and development. He is on a journey inward toward wholeness through emotional change effected in therapy and spiritual conversion gained by acceptance, courage and wisdom.

Integration as defined by Webster is the act of making a whole out of parts. My choice of using the aforementioned acronym is a figurative representation of just some of the qualities necessary for my integration as a pastoral counselor. It is only fitting that the first word integrity is, itself, a derivative of the word integer which is the whole of anything. Integrity means the state of being entire; a wholeness or-honesty. My whole concept of integration with respect to my clinical and theological studies at Neumann has and will continue to be directed toward wholeness. The process is a life-long task of developing my pastoral counseling skills and honing my talents one day at a time. The integration of cognitive therapy with Merton's theology is best illustrated by the following interaction: (378P) In other words if you are talking to your mother in the same situation where she puts the guilt trip on you It is alright to feel anger; not to verbalize anger to her.

She is your mother but to feel anger; to feel hurt. We are going back over this again. I don't know, would it pay to sometimes play those feelings out to the person. Would that work with regard to your mother (p.11)?

(385C) Naw! I don't think so. No! Not at this point. In this segment the devastation of the illusory or insidious nature of how the disease of alcoholism can impact upon a family and render this young man incapable of understanding his feelings let alone express them. I, openly confront Rob on the need for clarity and understanding in his life by the use of cognitive restructuring tools. I, also, point out to him the need for God's intervention through prayer in order to gain faith and hope (p.12, 1.386P- 397P). This is the movement from the false self to the true self; away from the dark shadow of repression and denial, toward the light of acceptance and rational understanding.

(398C) Rob responds, Yes, I guess. I don't know. It does bother me. It bothers me a lot seeing her like that, especially when, you know, I talk about drinking. It is not anger, it is frustration. It is like a build-up. It is not, I really like to yell at her. It's like you know -pull your hair out! I could like hit something. It is anger BUT it is more like frustration (p.16).

In this passage Rob is unsure what is frustration and what is anger and his inability to express anger is underscored. Rob is frustrated because he does not know what or how to feel. The repressed anger over his mother's alcoholic behavior coupled with conflicting guilt over the fact that he should not feel negative toward her since she is his mother, causes him much confusion and consternation. This frustration is unattended sows the seed for future alcoholic activity either as a co-dependent or a counter-dependent. The hurt and frustration negates positive change or growth and can lead to despair and self-destructive behavior. The false self is, indeed, addictive and will continue to stagnate upon its own immutable and sinister self.

The true self emerges when Rob begins to recognize his problems and then he deals with the reality of change for change heals. Using the cognitive model of rational responses, we see positive change in circumstances away from the false self of stagnation because that hurts and, thereby, stifles our spirit (p.12, 1.415P-422P) (432P)_ You are helping your mother in a way that only time will tell, Rob (p.13).

Sometimes in our desperation we become blinded to the significance of what is happening is not for our best interest. The changes as exemplified with Rob can be subtle thoughts or actions until one day his eyes will be opened to the truth and reality of positive growth and development through faith and trust.

Thomas Merton speaks of only finding your true self when you truly find God. When we dispel the illusory shadows of our false self by attending to our needs of the spirit (p.1, 1.6P) then we have integration. My clinical approach to the cognitive model (p.4, 1.113P) denotes the same careful and meticulous attention to the quest for integration by understanding how our mistaken belief systems or negative and automatic thoughts adversely impact on our well-being. Dysfunctional thoughts or cognitions cannot be identified, reality-tested or corrected until such time as thinking and acting more realistically and adaptively become integrated within the framework of learned experiences through the use of a variety of cognitive and behavioral strategies (ps.4-5, 1.125P-134P), (p.9-10, 1.305P-311P).

When we speak about integration as the coming together of certain qualities toward wholeness, our individual gifts of health, humor, intelligence among others. It must be interwoven with God's natural gifts for all of us. The gift of life, the gift of love, the gift of reason, the gifts of the Holy Spirit have and will be given to us if we only cooperate with his Divine Grace. In my opinion the greatest gift that I have received is the gift of my soul. I have been called from nothingness by the power of God to serve Him and love my neighbor as myself. Only by the successful integration of all of our individual and natural gifts can we accomplish this end. The act by which God creates us is an act of infinite love and calls for the gift of gratitude for the gift of life and being. (p.9, 1.284P-286P)

I trust that God's intention is for us to be whole and complete and by our daily struggles with life, we grow and discover the vastness of the mystery of who we are. Rob suffered deeply when his alcoholic mother exclaimed to him, Do you know what you, kids, "What are doing to me"? (340C) I try not to say anything to her because then I do, we start arguing...I really do not like your drinking and I will say stuff like that. She then slammed the door on me (p.10).

Discovery of self is a life-long endeavor complicated by self-deception. Illusion is the path of the false self which leads away from the true self. A dear and old friend, Fr. M, my spiritual director, who knows my strong and weak points. He continually affirms and accepts me for what I am. He helps me to experience myself as he sees me. He does not gloss over my undesirable foibles but instead accepts me in my totality.

When I, in turn, forget myself for others and accept them unconditionally then I realize the power for doing some good (p.14, 1.358P-369P).

As I begin to realize that I who am the source of good and love for others must somehow be good and lovable myself. Through this conversion experience and personal integration I grow day by day using life's petty annoyances and vexations a stepping stones not stumbling blocks for the greater good of my client(s) and myself.

<u>PASTORAL</u> COUNSELOR - A PERSONAL DEFINITION

"Lord, grant me the Serenity to accept the things I cannot change, the Courage to change the things I can, and the Wisdom to know the difference."

St. Francis of Assisi's prayer for serenity embodies all aspects of what it means for me to be a "pastoral counselor". I trust that I fit the mold of His Divine Plan. A clay pot does not ask the man who made it, "Why did you make me like this?" "After all, the man who makes the pots has the right to use the clay as he wishes, and to make two pots from the same lump of clay, one for special occasions and the other for ordinary use" (Romans 9:20,21). Not so long ago I felt like a miserable failure mired in hopelessness with virtually no self-esteem. As Fr. John Powell S.J. wrote:

"...a sense of personal worth is the backbone of human identity and the essential foundation of human happiness" (Powell, 1989, p.9).

I have learned from my own addiction to alcohol and years of cognitive therapy that a lack of sense of meaning and self-worth causes an impaired life adjustment. This becomes a marked dysfunction in the inner life of an alcoholic placing a spiritual problem at the heart of the disease's etiology. Full recovery requires holistic treatment and a rebuilding of one's life towards wellness. Surrender or the acceptance of things is essential to recovery but abstinence is unrealistic as the singular goal. We, alcoholics, are reborn when we become unable to accept the suffering of the disease and then we choose to escape the torment. We must "LET GO and LET GOD". Addictions can be transcended - not terminated. If a more conscious search for meaning does not begin in the alcoholic. We would not be able to prevent the addictive tendencies of power and control from overwhelming us. Something more subtle is needed;

it is created by the search for meaning and a spiritual awakening. That response to a higher quality of life is necessary. Without that help I can never be-united within myself. It is really a voluntary surrender to a HIGHER POWER. It transcends and can transform the false self to the true self. It is not a spontaneous conversion. It is based upon a new belief. It is rather an arduous ascent toward awakening. Only a blind man needs to believe that the sky is blue; a man who sees knows. The pastoral counselor that I define is a blend of acceptance, courage and wisdom. The acceptance of ourselves, others and God's Will; the courage to change ourselves for what is right and good; the wisdom to discern through self-acceptance and self-knowledge and unconditional love and forgiveness for all. It is the formula for my serenity and continued sobriety.

Albert Schweitzer once said and I paraphrase his remark. The greatest discovery of any generation is that human beings can change their lives by changing their attitudes of mind. We can sometimes miss seeing our inner goodness as I did for years because of a propensity for wanting more of the mundane. Perfectionists are rarely satisfied. We struggle with what's missing, not on what's found, what didn't get accomplished rather than what we did.

In pastoral counseling I have found that the emerging self from awareness to acceptance is a process; that there is now and that is okay, but there is, also, growth and development. Certain places in my soul seem most need of repair and they are, precisely, the places where I can connect with others - in their brokenness. Alcoholism is my disease; Our Lord is the Healer; Pastoral Counseling is the prescription toward wholeness.

The creative consequence of all of this is death and resurrection. As a recovering alcoholic and an aspiring pastoral counselor my illusory self must die but will be reborn again in the spirit of God. The alcoholic must quiet his soul and surrender to his Higher Power. The alcoholic who is in sober recovery realizes that he is not the center of the universe and he can't control his life. At the very point of his vulnerability is where the surrender takes place and that is when God enters. God comes in through the suffering of the soul and the wound of the alcoholic is laid open to the grace of God's loving care again and again. My ultimate objective is to accept my clients in same unconditional manner in which I have accepted disease of alcoholism and to apply lovingly my personal definition of **PASTORAL COUNSELING: SERENITY to accept my client wholly, COURAGE**

to effect change for growth, WISDOM to understand the real dynamics of the therapeutic alliance.

My identity as a pastoral counselor was, indeed, shaped by my experience at Neumann College and the loving and helpful assistance from the pastoral counseling staff and my fellow students. It is a continuing journey toward wholeness.

When I began as a neophyte in 1985, my life was beginning to unravel from the conflicting aspects of my addiction and prior years of dysfunctional thinking and acting out behavior. I was searching for something meaningful but I did not know for what I was searching. Now I do! Finally, the reality of change after years of emotional pain and suffering has given meaning to my life. The ongoing transformation is directly related to my experience at Neumann College. As Barbara P. could attest: that on so many occasions I just wanted to quit the program but an inner voice kept on driving me to endure. I continued to come back from my detours along the way and my journey to wholeness perseveres. This has taken courage and conviction in the face of adversity and apathy. THANKS NEUMANN! You shaped my identity.

CONCLUSION

A special tribute to the following:

Dr. Bob W, my first professor in Pastoral Counseling I and II who taught me unconditional regard, acceptance and availability for my clients. DR. Rick P. my first advisor and professor in group dynamics who taught me the importance of humor, good nature and the ability to be relaxed and be yourself.

Dr. Joann C, a dedicated professor who taught me the value of spirituality and personal maturity.

Dr. Rick V, a professor and mentor who in his untiring way has inspired to self-awareness and emerging self-acceptance. He celebrates with me in my "becoming".

Mrs. Barb P, a friend and secretary extraordinaire who has been there from the beginning. Your understanding, kindness, and friendly persuasion kept me going.

In closing, a message from John Powell S.J. "If you go after happiness directly, it will elude you. It's like trying to catch a butterfly. Run after it, and the butterfly will flutter away, but calm down and give your attention to something else and the beautiful butterfly is apt to land on your shoulder" (Powell, 1989, p.29). What a marvelous dual message for meaning. We have the butterfly whose essence represents change and we have the calming influence of peace and tranquility.

This is a statue of the Sacred Heart.
He has been my inspiration

My family on our 50ᵗʰ Wedding Anniversary

Caption: My youngest granddaughter,
Paige in on the beach.

Caption: A picture with no light other
than a miraculous Sun Ray 😇

Caption: My aspiring nurses are my granddaughters,
niece in the middle Caitlyn,Natalie,Catherine

Caption: Triplets, Catherine, Stephen,
Ryan are on the right, 1st yr,PITT

HEART VS BRAIN
concept

BIBLIOGRAPHY

Bailey, Joseph. Serenity Principle: Finding Inner Peace in Recovery, San Francisco:

Harper & Row, 1990

Beck, Aaron. Cognitive Therapy and the Emotional Disorders. New York: Basic Books, Inc., 1976

Beck, Aaron. Cognitive Therapy of Personality Disorders. New York: Basic Books, Inc., 1990

Burns, David M. D. Feeling Good. New York: William Morrow & Co., 1980

Fenhagen, James. Invitation to Holiness. San Francisco: Harper & Row, 1985

Finley, James. Merton's Palace of Nowhere. Ave Maria, 1985

Merton, Thomas. Contemplative Prayer. New York: Herder, 1969

Contemplation in a World of Action. New York Doubleday and Company, 1971

Mc Donnell, Thomas. Through the Year with Thomas Merton: Daily Mediations. New York: Image Books, 1985

Powell, John S. J. Happiness Is an Inside Job. California: Tabor Books, 1989

Stromberg, Clifford. The Psychologist's Legal Handbook.

The Council for the National Register of Health Service Providers in Psychology, 198West, Morris. The Shoes of the Fisherman. New York: William Morrow & Co., 1966

MY PRAYERS, SENTIMENTS AND THOUGHTS 🙏

My expressed intention of this book is reaching out to my fellow alcohol and drug folks who need help and support. Remember, we are not bad people. We are good people, but sick and tired who desire change and hope from the vestiges of drug addiction. We strive to live one day at a time in a sober and sane condition.

I am grateful and blessed by my Maker who answered my prayers along with family and friends.

Each day is a struggle, but my stepping stones are not stumbling blocks. I am eternally grateful to my wife, Rita, who is my soulmate. She has been my enabler in a good sense, a nurturer to me and my family, a bacon of light who shines a directed beam on my shortcomings.

It took years to understand her methods. I was frustrated by her simplicity. Rita is organized and disciplined. As my addiction intensified along with my resentment, rage and rebellion against her, I castigated her without merit.

In my recovery and each day, I understand her and my blame towards her has been replaced by acceptance, gratitude and wisdom. In the past, I wanted to be a true self but I was acting out in my false self and in Rita, I found my true self. In marriage we understand that we are one. It's a paradox, but we understand that in spiritual matters, we discern the truth which is elusive, but I learned that her truth self was my truth self. I found my true self in recovery and Rita was God's instrument. God speaks to us in people, places or things.

I give much credit to Rita, our married children and their spouses, our 10 loving grandchildren, give credit to my parents, aunts and uncles who gave me guidance and values. I give credit to my four siblings and their families. I thank my friends and I thank and pray for my people in particular that I offended.

In particular, I dedicate this book to my deceased nephew, Gerard, age 35 who died suddenly years back. Gerard was a very smart, personable and caring young man. My youngest son, David is the same age of Gerard who was born three days apart. I couldn't help Gerard and emotional issues overwhelmed him. He lived in Florida and I knew he had serious anxiety and depression issues, but he lost hope. I loved him and he is in a better place.

My remembrance of him and his legacy is inculcated in this book and each ripple in the sea is a cause and effect. We are bound by each other and once we become separated or lost, we become driftless and troubled waters immerse our bodies and souls. But, don't lose hope because our Good God will carry us away to a Safe Harbor.

Phil K, the Truthseeker🖤